Debbie Bedinger

Critical Incident Stress Management (CISM):

Grief Following Trauma

1st Edition

Authors:
Kevin L. Ellers, M.Div.
Nancy Rikli, M.S.
H. Norman Wright, M.R.E, M.A.

© January 2006, The International Critical Incident Stress Foundation, Inc., a nonprofit, nongovernmental organization in special consultative status with the Economic and Social Council of the United Nations. All rights reserved. Reproduction in any form is strictly prohibited without the prior written permission of the publisher.

Y0-BBY-709

INTERNATIONAL
CRITICAL
INCIDENT
STRESS
FOUNDATION

© January 2006, The International Critical Incident Stress Foundation, Inc., a nonprofit, nongovernmental organization in special consultative status with the Economic and Social Council of the United Nations. All rights reserved. Reproduction in any form is strictly prohibited without the prior written permission of the publisher.

All rights reserved.

For more information, contact ICISF at:
3290 Pine Orchard Lane, Suite 106
Ellicott City, Maryland 21042
(410) 750-9600
(410) 750-9601 fax
web site: www.icisf.org
EMERGENCY (410) 313-2473

ISBN 0-9765815-7-4

DEDICATION

To the many caregivers who dare to cross the line to enter the world of the hurting and also suffer the secondary effects of walking alongside the wounded in their journey of grief.

About the Authors

Kevin Ellers, M.Div.
Kevin is the Territorial Disaster Services Coordinator for The Salvation Army in the U.S.A. Central Territory. He is also president of the Institute for Compassionate Care which is dedicated to education, training and direct care. He serves as faculty for the International Critical Incident Stress Foundation, is a member of the American Association of Christian Counselors Training Team, and teaches broadly in the topics of Medic First Aid, grief, trauma, disasters, and emotional and spiritual care. Kevin is a candidate for the Doctor of Ministry degree in the Marriage and Family Therapy track and is currently working on the final project for completion of the degree. He has a strong background in disasters, chaplaincy, pastoral ministries, crisis intervention, grief and trauma care, marriage and family therapy and social services.

Nancy Rikli, M.S.
Nancy is the Director of Family Care Services of D.W. Newcomer's Sons Funeral Homes. She has master's degrees in Social Gerontology and Counseling Psychology. She is a certified trainer for Traumatic Grief, is certified as a Grief Counselor and a Trauma Specialist. Nancy is faculty for the International Critical Incident Stress Foundation and teaches broadly on the topics of crisis intervention and grief. Nancy is the founder of the Trauma Support Network in Kansas City, a member of the Kansas City Child Traumatic Stress Program, and the Suicide Awareness and Prevention Program.

H. Norman Wright, M.R.E., M.A.
H. Norman Wright is a licensed Marriage, Family and Child Therapist. He is a certified trauma specialist and traumatologist. He was former director of the Graduate Department of Marriage, Family and Child Counseling at Biola University, as well as an associate professor of Christian Education and Director of the Graduate Department of Christian Education at the Talbot School of Theology. He currently serves as faculty for the International Critical Incident Stress Foundation. He was in private practice for over thirty years. He is the author of over 75 books including: *The New Guide to Crisis and Trauma Counseling, Recovering from the Losses of Life, and Experiencing Grief*. He conducts grief recovery seminars nationally for communities and debriefings for various agencies. He also conducts training for the Victim Chaplain Association of America as well as other agencies.

TABLE OF CONTENTS

Authors' Note:
The content of this workbook is provided as a set of general guidelines only. The course or workbook is not intended to be used as a self-help manual, nor as a substitute for psychotherapy or professional mental health guidance. When in doubt, always consult a licensed mental health professional. Similarly, this manual may not be used as a substitute for formal training, supervision, or field experience.

The content of this course may be emotionally distressing to some participants. Participants are encouraged to leave the training at any point should they find the material excessively distressing. The instructor will be available to the participants during the training to discuss any adverse reactions to the course material, should this occur.

SECTION I

Introduction, Defining Terms & Self-Assessment

 # Critical Incident Stress Management: Grief Following Trauma

Course Description:

In the course of nearly everyone's life, they will, at some time, encounter grieving people following trauma or loss. This course is designed to help people develop a basic understanding of how to help grieving people following trauma. Course content includes how to identify characteristics of trauma and traumatic events, the normalcy of traumatic grief reactions, learn helpful death notification and body identification techniques, become skilled at identifying warning signs of complications, and learn the importance of early interventions and support utilizing the SAFER-R model. Participants will increase their knowledge of how trauma impacts the grief process and will gain skills for evaluating and supporting persons who have experienced traumatic loss. Upon completion, participants will be able to: identify types of traumatic events and the characteristics of trauma and grief; describe normal responses to trauma and normal grief responses; describe factors that may complicate the traumatic grief process; learn practical and effective methods of death notification and preparation for body identification; identify the primary needs of people experiencing grief following trauma; outline techniques for supporting people grieving a trauma; and self-care assessment and techniques. *(14 Contact Hours; 14 CE Credits for Psychologists; 14 CE Hours for Calif. MFTs & LCSWs; 14 Contact Hours for National Certified Addiction Counselors OR 1.4 General CEUs from UMBC)(Pending Approval:14 PDHs for EAPs;16.8 Nursing Contact Hours).* Completion of the "Grief Following Trauma" class and receipt of a certificate indicating full attendance (14 Contact Hours) qualifies as a class in ICISF's Certificate of Specialized Training Program.

Target Audience:

This course is designed for caregivers who work with people who experience grief and loss following a traumatic event.

Course Objectives:

By the end of the course the participant will be able to:
1. Identify types of traumatic events and the characteristics of trauma and grief.
2. Identify normal and pathological grief responses.
3. Describe factors that may help or hinder the traumatic grief process.
4. Perform essential skills for assisting grieving people including: death notification, preparing people for body identification, and effective support services.
5. Apply a practical application of the SAFER model to Rando's theory of the grief process.
6. Review techniques for supporting grieving people and identify resources for linking them to continued care.
7. Complete a personal loss and trauma history and develop a personal self-care plan.

> "To study psychological trauma is to come face to face both with human vulnerability in the natural world, and with the capacity for evil in human nature. To study psychological trauma means bearing witness to horrible events" Judith Herman, (2002)

Prevalence of Complicated Mourning

According to the United States Center for Disease Control (2002), there are approximately 2 million deaths annually in the USA and the life expectancy is at 77.3 years. Based on the figures that each individual death affects from 8–10 family members, it is calculated that are 16 to 20 million new mourners each year (Redmond, 1989).

After an extensive literature review, Raphael (1983) estimates that as many as one in three bereavements result in "morbid outcomes or pathological patterns of grief" (p.64). Application of this statistical outcome would indicate that potentially, 5-6 million new cases of complicated mourning annually (Rando, 1993).

These statistics may not take into account others touched by the death including neighbors, friends, co-workers, students or others outside the immediate family. In light of these affected individuals, some would argue that these numbers would be significantly higher.

Impact of Traumatic Grief

Too often we hear phrases such as "Time heals all wounds," or "It will get better with time." While life does continue after death for the bereaved, and this may generally be true, people may be surprised to find that as time passes, their grief and symptoms may intensify as indicated in the studies below. Time does not necessarily heal although it may alter one's perspective. It is what is done during this time and the way in which one mourns that makes a difference in the healing process following loss. Helping people to prepare for what they may experience in the years following death and loss can be a powerful tool to building resiliency and coping strategies

Research indicates that individuals bereaved from sudden and unexpected death may be impacted in the following ways:

- It takes at least a year to resume a normal pattern of daily life (Lehman and Wortman, 1987).

- A study of 110 couples whose child had been killed (many were subjects from Mother's Against Drunk Drivers), the study revealed that the second year was easier but the third year was worse. There were increases in intensity years three, five and seven, followed by a steady decrease (Ditchick, 1990). However others find that year two may be worse because grievers do not expect it to be so bad (Rinear, 1988).

- Bereaved individuals often visit their physicians more frequently and have more hospital admissions than the non-bereaved. They also generally suffer more depressive illnesses, anxiety states, personality disorders, rheumatic and arthritic conditions, disturbances of autonomic functions, and ulcerative colitis, and die more often than non-bereaved (Parkes, 1981).

- Traumatic loss and death is found to have significant impact upon children and youth who reported more depression, higher levels of global psychological stress, lower individuation from the family, and more difficulty forming intimate relationships than those who had experienced normal loss (Bradach, 1995).

- One study indicates that parents who lost adult children in vehicular crashes suffered more over-all psychiatric distress, guilt, and health complaints than parents whose children died of cancer (Schanfield, et.al., 1987).

- One study of 1447 bereaved and injured victims of drunk driving crashes showed that the greatest time of unmet support needs was one year after the death. Five years later, the test group was still significantly more stressed than non-victims on measures of well-being, somatization, obsessive-compulsion, depression, anxiety, hostility, self-esteem and PTSD. They also reported poorer health, were more likely to take more sleep medication or anti-anxiety drugs than non-victims (Mercer, 1993).

- The way that bereaved individuals interact in their world often changes post death. In one study, 49% of family members whose loved one was killed by a drunk driver and 36% of family members of someone murdered said that they were now much more careful about personal safety, began wearing seat belts, obeyed traffic laws, drove defensively, kept doors and windows locked, and 1% started carrying a gun (Amick-Kilpatrick, 1989).

Individual Reflection Exercise

Too often we fail to consider the scope of the impact of our life on others. Identify the social circles you are involved in and consider the circles of impact that your sudden death would impact. Identify a rough estimate of the number of people it would **significantly** impact.

Defining Characteristics of Trauma

In the left column, define the elements that make these incidents/events traumatic. List types of traumatic incidents/events in the right column. Give careful consideration to those incidents that may not be readily recognized by society.

Elements That Make It Traumatic	Traumatic Incidents/Events

Bereavement

Defining Grief

Reflect on your personal experience of grief and grieving people and write your own definition of grief below.

Mourning

Clinical Implications of Grief

Many people consider grief as an emotional reaction to a loss. However, grief clearly is far greater than just the emotional impact. Rando (1993) notes that there are five important clinical implications associated with the definition of grief:

- Grief is experienced in four major ways:

  o Psychologically: affects, cognitions, perceptions, attitudes, and philosophy, spirituality;

  o Behaviorally: personal action, conduct, or demeanor;

  o Socially: reactions to and interactions with others; *the world*

  o Physically: bodily symptoms and physical health. *Memory*

- Grief is a continuing development, is not a static state, but rather involves many changes with time.

- Grief is a natural, expectable reaction. The absence of grief, when warranted by the factors circumscribing the loss, is abnormal and indicative of pathology.

- Grief is a reaction to all types of loss, not just death. Death is only one example of loss, even though it may be the most dramatic, visible, and socially acknowledged loss.

- Grief is dependant upon the individual's unique perceptions of loss. It is therefore not necessary for the loss to be socially recognized or validated by others for the individual to grieve. However, it is helpful to the grief process when the acknowledgement and support is there.

As you listen to the survivors tell their stories in the video clips write below the symptoms within the categories listed below. Common categories of impact experienced by grievers include the following:

Physically:

Emotionally:

Cognitively:

Behaviorally:

Interpersonally:

Spiritually:

Loss Following Trauma and Death

We grieve because _____. It is important that one recognize that loss and grief are not just tied to death. We must consider the many other losses that occur that people must grieve and yet may not be socially acknowledged as a significant loss. When this happens, the griever may feel isolated and alone with his or her grief and lack the support that often accompany readily acknowledged losses such as sudden and unexpected deaths.

As a society, the physical loss that occurs is usually readily recognized. When one is robbed or a house is burned to the ground, the loss is observed and insurance may pay for the loss. When people die unexpectedly, people are shocked and recognize the loss. However, there are other losses that occur that may not be so readily recognized.

Reflection Exercise

Please take a few minutes to identify losses that may occur that may not be recognized or acknowledged.

While people often associate loss with death, one may suffer multiple losses resulting from a primary loss. In addition to the primary losses, there are also secondary losses that may be even greater than the primary loss. Mitchell & Anderson (1983) identify six major types of loss.

Material Loss: *The loss of a physical object or of familiar surroundings to which one has an important attachment.*

Relationship Loss: *The ending of opportunities to relate oneself to, talk with, share experiences with, make love to, touch, settle issues with, fight with, and otherwise be in the emotional and/or physical presence of a particular other human being.*

Intrapsychic Loss: *The experience of losing an emotionally important image of oneself, losing the possibilities of "what might have been," abandonment of plans for a particular future, the dying of a dream. Although often related to external experiences, it is itself an entirely inward experience.*

Functional Loss: *The loss of bodily functioning such as muscular or neurological functions.*

Role Loss: *The loss of a specific social role or of one's accustomed place in a social network is experienced as role loss.*

Systemic Loss: *Human beings are relational beings who belong to some interconnected system in which patterns of behavior develop over time. The absence of members or change within the systemic structure may significantly and permanently alter the system.*

Defining Impact

Society often quickly defines who is most impacted by a traumatic event, loss or bereavement in ways which excludes certain people who are greatly impacted. It is critical that caregivers give careful consideration to those who may be missed in an initial assessment of impact.

Victim:

Survivor:

Co-victim:

Secondary victimization:

Ambiguous Loss

- Physically absent but psychologically present

- Physically present but psychologically absent

Ambiguous loss is difficult because (Wright, 2003):

- There can be confusion and difficulty identifying the problem

- There may be uncertainty which prevents people from adjusting to the ambiguity of their loss

- People may be denied the rituals that ordinarily support a defined loss

Disenfranchised Grief

Disenfranchised grief may be characterized as a *loss that cannot be openly acknowledged, publicly mourned or socially supported.*

Three types of disenfranchised grief:

- Relationships that are not recognized or socially sanctioned

- The loss is not recognized as significant

- The griever is not recognized (Doka, 1989)

Trauma and Loss Exercise

Working with traumatized and grieving people can stir up significant feelings and thoughts within caregivers. It is critical that we have an understanding of the situations, incidents, and population groups that may trigger these internal reactions. Take some time to start the exercise below. You will not have time to complete this in class but can continue to work on this after the class.

NOTE: You will not be asked to show this to anyone or share details. However, you will summarize what you have learned from this exercise with another person as relates to working with traumatized and grieving people.

Part One:
Complete a trauma and loss timeline on the next page by recording significant incidents that have impacted your life. Start at birth and continue to today. Write the trauma or loss at the top and the primary and secondary losses and impact at the bottom. Consider how you grieved each incident.

TODAY

BIRTH

Part Two: Identify situations or population groups of which you need to be aware as they serve as internal triggers for you.

Situations, external stimuli, and population groups which serve as internal triggers are…	It triggers…

SECTION II

Elements of Normal & Traumatic Grief

Traumatic Events and the Brain

Why it matters

Following a traumatic incident, crisis responders and caregivers need to understand the human response to traumatic events in order to help survivors prepare for what they will experience and help them learn ways to cope. Information is empowering to survivors as it allows them to take an active role in the recovery process. Survivors often fail to understand why they behaved in certain ways during and following the traumatic event and may struggle with guilt because of their thought, feelings, or behaviors. Helping them to understand common stress reactions is important.

It is important to help survivors understand that although people's reactions to stress, disasters, and traumatic events vary widely, clinical researchers have identified common patterns of behavioral, biological, psychological, spiritual, and social responses (see appendix).

Also important is to highlight that while the stress reactions that survivors may experience may seem "extreme," feel abnormal and cause distress, they generally do not become chronic problems. The research indicates that most people fully recover from moderate stress reactions within 6-16 months. While survivors may experience post traumatic stress symptoms, only fraction of these people will experience post traumatic stress disorder (PTSD) (Breslau, Davis, Andreski, & Peterson, 1991); Elliott, 1997; Kulka et.al., 1990).

Emergency response and mental mobilization

The complex infrastructure and inner workings of the human body regulated by a relatively small brain is an awesome and amazing system that allows adequate functioning within diverse situations. This is perhaps no more evident than in the brain which controls and coordinates all elements of the human body. Traumatic and threatening events have a significant impact upon the brain and the resulting physical and emotional reactions. Perry and Pollard (1998) state: "Although exquisitely complex, the core framework of the human brain is designed to sense and respond to the changing environment to promote survival" (p. 36).

In emergency situations the brain activates an enhanced cognitive state of mental mobilization to face imminent threat and sustain survival (Dyregrov, Solomon, and Bassoe, 2000). At each level of the central nervous system (CNS) the input is interpreted and matched against previous similar patterns of activation. To survive, the body's stress response system kicks in to meet the perceived threat. Thus each level and area of the brain activates as needed to face the critical incident. A brief summary of these key components are as follows (Dyregrov, et al, 2000):

Brainstem: The brainstem represents the most basic of functions which regulates the autonomic and hypothalamic output, alters arousal, and tunes out distracting sensory information.

<u>Midbrain</u>: The midbrain regulates elements of motor activity (e.g., the startle response).

<u>Limbic System</u>: The limbic system modulates emotional reactivity and signaling (e.g. facial expression).

<u>Cerebral Cortex</u>: The cerebral cortex interprets the threat and develops a complex plan.

Ideally these multiple responses serve as an integrated and orchestrated process to mobilize a host of actions that will result in adaptive functioning, risk reduction, and will enhance survival. There are a number of critical mechanisms of mental mobilization as an outcome of this activation including (Dyregrov, et al., 2000):
- Enhanced sensory awareness;
- focused attention;
- rapid processing of incoming data;
- enhanced memory;
- altered time perception;
- use of relevant past knowledge;
- and temporary deactivation of emotional reactions.

It is important for caregivers in traumatic situations to have a good understanding of this process to help survivors understand their reactions and the accompanying responses to come. It is common for survivors to depict their perception of how things appeared to move in slow motion and may believe that they moved more slowly than they should have, rather than understanding that the mind rapidly speeds up to process the data and meet the perceived threat. A sharpening of one's senses and an increased hypervigilence may also occur, neither of which feels normal to the survivor. Because there is often a temporary deactivation of emotional reactions, a survivor may also feel guilt for a lack of emotional reaction. An integral part of effective mental mobilization is the temporary deactivation of emotional reactions. This ability to block emotions for short or long periods of time, allow information processing and survival mechanisms to work without being overwhelmed. The shock reactions postpone emotional reactions to allow one to handle the event as it unfolds and experience the event a little at a time. This also describes the frequent feelings of unreality, dream-like, or movie-like experience. As will be discussed later in this course, allowing people to tell their story in a safe environment helps them to "make it real" and grounds them in reality. It also provides an opportunity for caregivers to normalize these reactions, which in turn greatly assist in the healing process (Dyregrov, et al., 2000).

Hemispheric Specialization

Clinical and experimental research of the brain has led to the dual brain theory. The brain consists of two halves. There is a constant flow of information from one hemisphere to the other. The dual brain theory poses three major points: (1) each hemisphere governs the actions of the opposite side of the body. (The right side of the brain controls the left side of the body; the left side of the brain controls the right side of the body.) (2) The left hemisphere processes logical and analytical information by thinking in words, numbers and symbols. The right side processes spatial, holistic, and nonverbal information by thinking in pictures and images. (3) Each side of the brain collects certain types of information to control behavior based on that information. The major functions for each hemisphere are as follows (Wolvin, 1982):

Left Hemisphere	Right Hemisphere
Verbal: reading, writing, speaking, and listening to verbal messages; thinking in words or symbols	*Nonverbal*: projecting and perceiving non verbal cues
Linguistic: being competent in the grammar, syntax, and semantics of language	*Nonlinguistic*: seeing objects, events, etc., as they are without names/words connected to them; lacking the linguistic elements of grammar, syntax, and semantics
Analytical: reducing the whole to its parts	*Holistic*: seeing in wholes
Logical/rational: reasoning	*Emotional*: responding to/with feeling
Mathematical/digital: computing, measuring, and timing	*Intuitive*: having insight; responding with "ah ha" premonitions
Linear: perceiving objects, events, etc., in their true relation to one another	*Creative*: exhibiting inventiveness/imagination
Syntactical: arranging information in an orderly/systematic manner	*Special/relational*: recognizing patterns, configurations, shapes, forms, etc., even though part of the data may be missing
Objective: being independent of mind	*Perceptual*: seeing in three dimensions; having depth perception
Articulate: expressing oneself clearly/distinctly	*Visual*: thinking in images/pictures
Ordered: organizing; categorizing information	*Artistic*: having skill in such activities as art, music, dance
Aesthetic: enjoying stimuli	*Novel*: responding to new/unknown stimuli; being innovative

The two sides of the brain are connected by the corpus callosum which serves as the mechanism for communication between the right and left hemispheres. Because women have up to 40 percent more of these nerve bundles than men, they are better able to more fully utilize both sides of their brains at the same time (Wright, 2003). Men often have to switch focus from one side of the brain to the other, depending upon the nature of the task being performed. Women can enjoy more cross-talk between both sides of the brain since they use their brains holistically. Women, may find it easier to handle multiple tasks at one time and often read earlier than boys. It is important to note that in order to derive the most out of life, people need the functions of both sides.

Three other key parts are the following:
1. Hypothalamus – Receives incoming information through our senses' sight, smell, hearing, touch and taste, then passes it on to other parts of the brain for processing.

2. Hippocampus – Interprets emotional valence (vigor); controls emotional response by transforming sensory stimuli into emotional and hormonal signals, then refers this information to other parts that control behavior.

3. Frontal Cortex – Acts as supervisory system of the whole process of integration of emotional and cognitive functions.

When the brain functions the way it's supposed to, the system functions well. However, traumatic events have the power to significantly change the brain's functioning. Trauma can cause a wounding to the bodily systems and may overwhelm the ordinary functioning modes. Trauma can create an altered state of functioning that can impair one's ability to perform essential tasks and frequently leads to psychological decomposition, or a "dumbing down" effect of cognitive impairment.

The brain's design allows it to function as a holistic unit to create balance and appropriate levels of functioning. Traumatic events that overwhelm one's ability to cope tend to create a separation and communication between brain components and an interruption of functioning. Thus, survivors may experience vivid graphic thoughts or images of the traumatic event with little or no emotion. The survivor may also experience intense emotions but without the thoughts or actual memories and an impaired ability to cognitively process these emotions.

The intrusiveness of traumatic events can be invasive, and may seem to temporarily take control of one's life. Survivors may find that they are washed back and forth between reliving the trauma, overwhelming floods of intense emotion, impulsive action, intrusive thoughts, involuntary physiological responses, and or numbness and immobilization.

There can also be long-term physical affects of trauma upon survivors. The hippocampus may be reduced in size which impacts memory, causing lapses in concentration and deficits in recall.

The higher systems of the brain such as the frontal cortex's ability may also be decreased. This creates a lessened ability to do basic left brain functions. Survivors may find a decreased ability to appropriately access danger and distinguish between real and false threats. It may also limit people from putting into words what they feel. Thus, survivors may have an increased startle response and hypervigilance, falsely perceiving that there is danger.

Intense stress or trauma is accompanied with the release of hormones and chemicals into the brain. Pathways running within the brain to the adrenal glands triggers adrenaline and noradrenaline secretions. Adrenaline and noradrenaline surge through the blood stream causing the heart to beat faster and prime the body for an emergency. These hormones then activate receptors on the vagus nerve running back to the brain. This causes the heart to continue to beat faster, but also signals various parts of the brain to supercharge a intense emotional memory. These hormones assist the individual to mobilize in the event of emergency. They also sweep through the body, return to the brain, and trigger the release of more equally powerful hormones (cortisol, epinephrine and norepinephrine, oxytocin, vasopressin and endogenous opioids). This flood of hormones produces the "fight-flight" response in people.

When a threat is perceived and the body prepares to respond to an emergency, the heart beats faster, blood pressure increases, and breathing speeds up pumping maximum levels of oxygen and energy-rich blood to the muscles. The liver releases more sugar into the blood to prepare for immediate response in the face of danger. However, for some individuals, it produces a freeze effect. When this occurs, these hormones which are rushing through the body and have no appropriate physical response as an outlet and the stressor paralyzes the victim. This freezing is call tonic immobility and is similar to a mouse going limp when caught by a cat, or stiff, like deer caught in a spotlight (Gallup & Maser, 1977).

In times of perceived threat, the brain functions in a different mode dumping an excess of chemicals which in the immediacy of the event can produce a "dumbing down" effect on the traumatized person. During this time, the caregiver can play a pivotal role in helping to stabilize survivors with objective thinking and a calming influence.

The Amygdala

The amygdala also plays a crucial role in the emotional center of the brain. The amygdala stores the emotions related to what is experienced. Thus, every experience that one has that evokes emotions, regardless of how subtle, appears to derive from an emotional reaction that is encoded within the amygdala (LeDoux, 1996).

Dr. Antonio Damasio, a neurologist at the University of Iowa, had a patient who was a brilliant corporate lawyer. This man had developed a small tumor in the prefrontal lobes which was surgically removed. The surgery was deemed successful with the exception that the surgeon accidentally cut the circuits connecting the lawyer's prefrontal lobes with the amygdala. The results were puzzling in that while the lawyer displayed no discernible cognitive deficits, he became inept at work, lost his job, and was unable to maintain employment. He ended up jobless, his wife left him, and he lost his home (Vogel, 1997) .

The prefrontal area of the brain is the location of the operational working memory. This allows a person to have the capacity to pay attention, maintain essential information, and is vital for comprehension, understanding, planning, decision making, reason and learning. When the mind is calm, this working memory functions at its best. However, in times of emergency, the brain shifts into a self protective mode, dumping chemicals into the brain and pirating resources from this brain area for use in other brain areas to keep the senses in a hyper alert status. This survival mechanism allows a person to focus on the perceived danger at hand.

The amygdala serves as the brain's memory bank and is a repository for all of our emotions including fear, anger, pleasure and hope. Thus the amygdala serves as sentinel, constantly processing everything that is taken in through the senses and assessing it for threats and opportunities by comparing the current situation with past experiences.

When the amygdala perceives danger and hits the panic button, it induces a cascade that begins with the release of chemical hormones known as CRF thus dumping a flood of stress hormones mostly consisting of cortisol (Duffy, J.D., 1997). These hormones that are released under stress are targeted for flight or fight in that circumstance, however, they stay in the body for hours, with additional stressful incidents increasing the levels of stress hormones. This can result in a buildup making individuals prone to an emotional hijack and hair trigger reactions of provocation, anger, or panic.

Stress hormones have an impact upon blood flow. As the heart rate increases, blood is shunted away from the brain's higher cognitive centers to other brain locations designed for emergency operations. Levels of blood sugar increase to provide fuel for immediate response and the body prepares itself for basic survival. The result is a dulling of the mind which causes people to revert that which is most familiar what is most rehearsed. In martial arts, students are forced to perform katas, which are basic defensive and offensive moves that with consent repetition become automatic when in a fight. In times of danger, emergency personnel often report an ability to quickly recall in detail prior training and automatically respond almost as if they are not connected with their behavior. This is one of the reasons that repetitive emergency response training is essential to successful functioning under increased stress levels.

If stress is maintained for extend periods of time it can cause negative physical, psychological and spiritual effects. When lab rats are put under constant strain, cortisol and related stress hormones reach toxic levels that poison and kill neurons. If the stressors continue over a significant part of their lifespan, there is a dramatic effect on the brain with an erosion and shrinkage of the hippocampus which is vital to memory (Vogel, 1997). Similar impacts of stress are observed in humans. The brain normally functions within a system of checks and balances. The prefrontal lobes ordinarily function in a manner so as to keep the amygdala's urges and raw impulses in check based on a cognitive processing in accordance with understanding the event within the larger context of life.

Because the amygdala serves as the brain's alarm, it has the power to override the prefrontal lobes within a split second to meet the emergency it identifies. However, the prefrontal lobes cannot quickly and directly override the amygdala. Instead, the prefrontal lobes have an array of inhibitory neurons that are capable of stopping the directives being frantically sent by the amygdala. This may be explained similar to how one would shut off the house false alarm by entering the secret code (Goleman, 1998).

A problem may occur when the next emergency arises. The physical, biological body remembers, and responds, the same way it did before, without any decision making process from the lessons learned by the intellectual brain in the last emergency. Traumatic events are remembered differently than non-traumatic events. These memories appear as if free floating in time and are experienced as "now" and not just a past event (Wright, 2003).

Building Personal Hardiness
In the impact stage following a traumatic event, disaster workers and pastoral caregivers can serve to provide a buffer for individuals by providing comfort, safety and clear thinking. This is an example of when the well worn phrase "two heads are better than one" applies.

Richard Davidson, the director of the Laboratory for Affective Neuroscience at the University of Wisconsin, conducted a landmark study of brain imaging that tested two groups of people. One group was identified as highly resistant to life's ups and downs and the other easily upset by them. Davidson tracked their brain function as they performed stressful tasks. The research revealed that that resilient people had a remarkably fast recovery from stress, with their prefrontal areas starting to calm the amygdala and themselves within seconds. By contract, the more vulnerable people saw a continued escalation of their amygdala's activity, and their distress, for several minutes after the activity ended (Sherman, 1994; Goleman, 1998).

Davidson found that the resilient people had already started to inhibit the distress during the stressful encounter. He identified these people to be optimistic, action-oriented people. These people faced life's stressors by immediately trying to make things better. A study of store managers at a large American retail chain found that the managers who were most tense, beleaguered, or overwhelmed by job pressures ran stores with the worst performance, as measured by: net profits, sales per square foot, sales per employee, and per dollar of inventory investment. However, interestingly, those who stayed the most composed under the same pressures had the best per-store sales records (Sherman, 1994).

TRAUMATIC EXPERIENCE	LOSS

TRAUMA
Impaired concentration
Reexperiencing, exaggerated startle
Recurrent recollections
Traumatic play
Somatic complaints w/ reminders
Traumatic dreams
Reenactment /recurrence
Distress w/ reminders
Numbing and avoidance
Efforts to avoid thoughts, feelings
Conversations, activities, people,
places, & activities
Diminished interest
Inability to recall aspects
Detachment from others
Restricted affect, hypervigilance
Foreshortened future
Arousal, sleep disturbance
Traumatic rage

INTERACTION
May intensify with
overlapping symptoms

Reminiscing/thoughts
Traumatic recollections
Traumatic aspects may hinder
or complicate grief work
relationship to deceased
issues of identification
processing anger/rage

Sense of estrangement
may interfere with
healing interactions

BEREAVEMENT
Disbelief/shock/numbness
Searching
Reunion wishes
Yearning
Reminiscing
Grief dreams
Grief play
Somatic reactions

Diminished interest or pleasure

Sadness

Sense of numbing while carrying
out routine actions

Sleep disturbance, impaired
concentration/anger/ irritability

(Adapted Nader, 2002)

Responses/Triggers

Stimulus Cued

Cyclic

Linear

Other

Scenario

As a crisis response team, you have been called in to work with an industrial plant in which an accident occurred. As a 2000 lb. piece of equipment that was being moved by a forklift began to fall, one of the workers stepped in front of the equipment to stop it and was crushed. He died instantly. The death was witnessed by 6 people. There has been a lot of guilt expressed by the bystanders who feel they should have been able to stop it from happening. In meeting with the employees, one witness expresses that he/she should have been able to stop the event because, in their words, "it happened in slow motion. I could see it moving and I knew it was going to happen. I should have been able to stop it but I just stood there. I am such an idiot. If I had just acted, he would have still been alive. It is all my fault." The event happened a week ago and he is experiencing many of the typical symptoms of post traumatic stress. S/he is scared by these new intrusive memories, feelings, thoughts, and the accompanying physical reactions and his/her inability to control them.

Your tasks

- **For the purpose of this exercise, just focus on the education component not other intervention skills.**

- Break into pairs.

- Pretend that your co-victim has just explained the scenario to you and you have engaged in active listening as s/he painted the trauma story to you.

- Practice doing a one-on-one brief education of some common trauma and grief symptoms they may experience based on what they witnessed.

- Your task is to sensitively and simply educate the bystander and help them prepare for what they may experience.

- To help with the guilt of lack of intervention, explain simply how mental mobilization occurs.

Common Responses to Trauma & Grief

A common mistake among the general public is a false perception about grief that relates primarily to emotional reactions and expression. Grief is all encompassing and touches the whole of our being and all facets of our lives.

Physical

Emotional

Behavioral

Mental

Interpersonal

Spiritual

GRIEF

A Tangled Ball of Emotions

Wright, 2003, p.111

Trauma Factors That Impact Grief

There are many factors that play a role in the griever's ability to grieve the loss and adjustment to the world without the deceased.

- Weiss (1986, 1988) identified specific factors correlating with complicated mourning including (1) an ambivalent relationship, (2) previous unresolved losses, (3) weakness in character, and (4) lack of a promising future.

- A study of 60 widows and widowers in their 60's found age to be the most significant predictor of high stress. The very young (25-30) and the elderly (66-85) experienced the highest stress (Steele, 1992).

- The level of internal feelings of control is an important factor. One study comparing 30 widowers and 30 widows with 60 married people found those with a weak internal locus of control who experiences the unexpected death of a spouse had higher levels of depression and somatic complaints with 42% clinically depressed at six months and 27% clinically depressed after two years (Strobe, Strobe & Domittner, 1988).

- The perception of one's support system is important to the coping abilities of the grieving person.

Suddenness

History

Relationship with the deceased

Coping skills

Support system (positive and negative aspects)

Faith system

Culture

Multiple events

Prior mental and physical health

Witness

Presence of the body

Prolonged events

Perception

Sudden, Unexpected Death

All death and trauma presents challenges unique to each situation. There are a number of issues that are inherent to sudden, unanticipated death that may significantly complicate the mourning process. Rando (1993) cites the following:

- The capacity to cope is diminished as the shock effects overwhelm the ego at the same time additional stressors are added.

- The assumptive world is violently shattered without warning and the violated assumptions cause intense reactions of fear, anxiety, vulnerability and loss of control.

- The loss does not make sense, and cannot be understood or absorbed.

- There is no chance to say good-bye and resolve unfinished business with the deceased, which cause problems due to the lack of closure.

- Symptoms of acute grief and of physical and emotional shock persist for a prolonged period of time.

- The mourner obsessively reconstructs events in an effort both to comprehend the death and to prepare for it in retrospect.

- The mourner experiences a profound loss of security and confidence in the world which affects all areas of life and increases many kinds of anxiety.

- The loss cuts across experiences in the relationship and tends to highlight what was happening at the time of death, often causing these last-minute situations to be out of proportion with the rest of the relationship and predisposing to problems with realistic recollection and guilt.

- The death tends to leave mourners with relatively more intense emotional reactions, such as great anger, ambivalence, guilt helpless, death anxiety, vulnerability, confusion, disorganization, and obsession with the deceased along with strong needs to make meaning of the death and to determine blame and affix responsibility for it.

- The death tends to be followed by a number of major secondary losses (Rando, 1984) because of the consequences of lack of anticipation.

- The death can provoke posttraumatic stress responses.

Factors that Impact the Grief Process

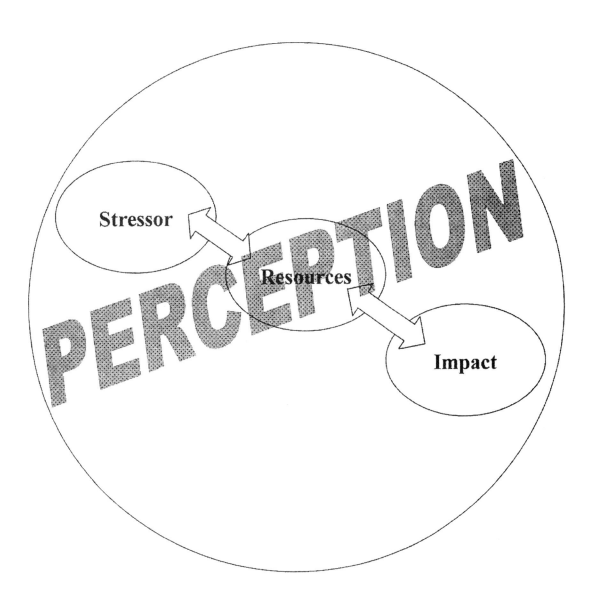

Notes:

SECTION III

Personality,
Grief & Mourning

Patterns of Grief

Well meaning caregivers sometimes fail to understand the different ways that people grief the losses in their lives. It is easy to approach another person through the eyes of one's own perspective and offer help that may not be beneficial to the unique grieving style and personality of the other person. Martin and Doka (2000) discuss two distinct patterns of grieving and a third blending of these two patterns. Their approach challenges the traditionally held, yet empirically unsupported notions of grief reactions and what is helpful to grieving people (Martin & Doka, 2000).

Instrumental Grievers	Intuitive Grievers
•Focus on cognition/moderated affect; while they share common feelings with intuitive grievers, feelings are less intense	•Focus on affect over cognition
•Brief periods of cognitive dysfunction are common	•Longer term cognitive impairment as there may be prolonged periods of confusion, inability to concentrate, disorganization, and disorientation
•A desire to master environment; thus a majority of grief energy is focused on problem-solving and planned activities as an adaptive strategy	•Are less likely than instrumental grievers to seek out potential problems and solve them
•A general reluctance to talk about feelings	•Feelings are intensely experienced
•Grief is more of an intellectual experience	•Expressions such as crying and lamenting mirror inner experience
•May initially respond by explaining the circumstance of their losses rather than to affective cues	•Grief expressed is a grief experienced

•Go with the experience of grief |
| •May experience grief physically as augmented energy and take the form of restlessness or nervousness | •Majority of grief energy is focused on feelings – less energy for cognition |
| •May be unaware of internal arousal | •Successful adaptive strategies facilitate the experience and expression of feeling

•Physical exhaustion and/or anxiety may result |
| •May feel disenfranchised as others do not accept their grief pattern | •May feel that people do not allow for adequate expression of their grief |
| •May be uncomfortable with the strong expressed emotions of others | •May be unable or unwilling to distance themselves from feelings expressed by others |

Blended Grievers

Blended grievers have elements common to both instrumental and intuitive patterns, but with a general preference for one. It is suggested that there are probably more blended grievers than intuitive or instrumental, with most leaning more toward the intuitive side. Since blended grievers express grief in way characteristic to both patterns, they benefit from a variety of adaptive strategies from which to select. They may or may not have sufficiently developed adaptive strategies in both areas. Sudden and unexpected deaths seem to exert their greatest influence with blended grievers as perception and interpretation of the loss play an important factor.

(Martin & Doka, 2000)

Instrumental Griever:

Intuitive Griever:

Blended Griever:

Grief Pattern Inventory

Please respond to each of the following statements using the key below. If appropriate, choose the response that best describes you in the past 2 weeks.

A	U	S	R	N
Always	Usually	Sometimes	Rarely	Never

A	U	S	R	N	
A	U	S	R	N	1. I am more emotional than most people I know.
A	U	S	R	N	2. It is easy for me to cry and show my feelings to others.
A	U	S	R	N	3. Even though I have returned to my normal routine, I still have strong and painful feelings about my loss.
A	U	S	R	N	4. Even though I feel like crying, I do not cry in front of others.
A	U	S	R	N	5. Although I am grieving in my own way, others may think me cold and unfeeling.
A	U	S	R	N	6. I don't seem to get as upset as most other people I know.
A	U	S	R	N	7. I feel overwhelmed by feelings of grief.
A	U	S	R	N	8. I appreciate when others encourage me to share my painful feelings with them.
A	U	S	R	N	9. I avoid highly emotional or "touchy-feely" situations of any kind.
A	U	S	R	N	10. It is important to me that others view me as being in control.
A	U	S	R	N	11. I have been told that I am avoiding my grief even through I don't think that I am.
A	U	S	R	N	12. I have been controlling my painful feelings by drinking or by using other prescription or nonprescription drugs.
A	U	S	R	N	13. I believe that a bereavement support group is (would be) very helpful for me.
A	U	S	R	N	14. I worry that I am not as upset by my loss as I should be, and feel guilty that I don't have more intense feelings.
A	U	S	R	N	15. I resent efforts to get me to show feelings that I don't have.
A	U	S	R	N	16. I *think* more about my loss than *feel* things about my loss.
A	U	S	R	N	17. I believe that it is very important to be aware of, and in touch with, all of my feelings.
A	U	S	R	N	18. I find that solving problems associated with my loss helps me.
A	U	S	R	N	19. Although I can sometimes control my painful feelings, they usually return and overwhelm me.
A	U	S	R	N	20. Since my loss, I feel like I'm just pretending to be strong in front of most people.
A	U	S	R	N	21. I find that I can't stop my grieving by thinking of other things.
A	U	S	R	N	22. I have taken deliberate action to honor the memory of my loved one, even though I have not been as upset as most others who are grieving my loved one.
A	U	S	R	N	23. Others seem surprised by my recovery from my loss.
A	U	S	R	N	24. Although I took care of things immediately after my loved one's death, I was surprised when I eventually "crashed" and began to have intense and painful feelings.
A	U	S	R	N	25. I would describe myself as more intellectual than emotional.

Used with permission from: Martin, T. L. & Doka, K. J. (2000) *Men Don't Cry...Women Do: Transcending Gender Stereotypes of Grief.* Philadelphia, PA: Brunner/Mazel.

Grief Pattern Inventory (GPI)
Item Analysis and Scoring Inventory

The GPI contains 25 items with response choices ranged along a continuum: always, usually, sometimes, rarely, and never. This reflects the belief that patterns exist on a continuum from profoundly intuitive to intensely instrumental. The GPI is designed to augment other methods of professional assessment in one's grief. In addition, it is always a sound practice to re-administer the GPI after several weeks have passed. Dissonant responses, in particular, are often temporary in nature. Finally, it is suggested that one wait at least two to three weeks after the death to begin evaluating patterns. Suggested guidelines for interpreting a griever's scores are as follows.

Scoring Key				
A = +2	U = +1	S = 0	R = -1	N = -2
Intuitive Pattern	Questions #: 1, 2, 3, 7, 8, 13, 17, 19, 21, 24			
Score	16-20	Profoundly intuitive pattern		
	11-15	Moderate intuitive pattern		
	6-10	Blended intuitive pattern		
	-5-+5	Blended balanced patterns		
Instrumental Pattern	Questions #: 5, 6, 9, 11, 15, 16, 18, 22, 23, 25			
Score	16-20	Profoundly instrumental pattern		
	11-15	Moderate instrumental pattern		
	6-10	Blended instrumental pattern		
	-5-+5	Blended balanced patterns		
Dissonant Responses	Questions #: 4,10,12,14, 20	Each dissonant response should be evaluated separately.		

Group Exercise
What Helps?

Now that you have completed the Grief Pattern Inventory (GPI), identify within your assigned group what helps and what does not help the Intuitive and Instrumental Grieving types. Complete the do and don't lists below:

Helping individuals with the instrumental preference:
Don't...   **Do...**

Helping individuals with the intuitive preference:
Don't...   **Do...**

Case Study Video

As you watch the video consider the following things and write your thoughts below:

- What was your internal reactions as you watched the videos?

- What caregiver actions helped Robert?

- What did Robert draw on for strength?

- What does this video indicate about Robert's faith?

- What did you observe about Robert's grief and mourning?

Notes:

SECTION IV

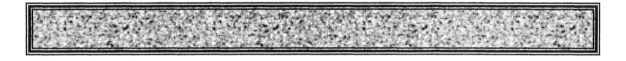

The Avoidance Phase

Grief as a Process

Human beings tend to want structure and order within their environment and often tend to try to fit processes within a defined structure to create a sense of comprehension, direction and order. However, there are problematic issues that arise when trying to broadly apply any set structure to the complex and varied individual journey following trauma and loss.

Kubler-Ross (1969) has one of the most known stage models from her work with dying patients. This model is frequently cited and applied by some in a broad attempt as the standard by which all grief should be assessed. It is important to note that this model was designed to be used in relation to one's own grief in facing one's own death and is frequently misapplied outside the intended context of the model.

Kubler-Ross – Five Stages of Loss

- Denial

- Anger

- Bargaining

- Depression

- Acceptance

With increasing research, the stage models are questioned and are perceived by some as perhaps more problematic than helpful when misapplied within the wrong context. There is a tendency to oversimplify a complex journey into several defined stages that may be viewed a linear progression that may not resonate with the grieving individual. There is no clearly consistent documented research that indicates that people go through a consistent set series of stages to experience "closure" or resolution. Grievers often cycle back through many previously experienced emotions, behaviors, and cognitions and experience recurrent grief symptoms. In fact, some people may find that their symptoms worsen with time after having experienced a lessening of emotional intensity of their grief.

Worden (1991) defines a popular model of the grief process in terms of the four tasks that the griever has to accomplish in the grief work.

Worden's 4 Tasks
▪ Accept the reality of the loss ▪ Work through the pain ▪ Adjust to an environment without the deceased ▪ Emotionally relocate the deceased and moving on

Therese Rando's (1993) extensive work, *Treatment of Complicated Mourning*, provides a comprehensive structure in which to overlay the CISM SAFER Model when working with grieving individuals.

Rando's Theory of the Grief Process

Avoidance Phase
- Recognize the loss

Confrontation Phase
- React to the separation

- Recollect and re-experience the deceased and the relationship

- Relinquish the old attachments to the deceased and the old assumptive world

Accommodation Phase
- Readjust to move adaptively into the new world without forgetting the old

- Reinvest

Throughout the class, participants should seek to define practical ways in which caregivers can assist grieving individuals. In reviewing the tasks or processes through which the grieving individual moves in the grief continuum, the CISM SAFER Model (Everly & Mitchell, 2003) will be applied to assist caregivers in defining practical ways of assisting grieving individuals.

CISM SAFER Model
▪ Stabilize
▪ Acknowledgment
▪ Facilitation of understanding
▪ Encouragement of adaptive coping
▪ Recovery/Referral

The Avoidance Phase
The initial aftermath following trauma or loss is a critical phase for caregivers working with grieving individuals. This is a period in which direct and simplistic care is critical in helping to provide stability and direction in the chaos that may occur.

Recognizing the Loss
- Diverse reactions

- Shock as a natural coping mechanism and psychological buffer

- Denial

- Importance of a sensitive and appropriately completed death notification

SECTION V

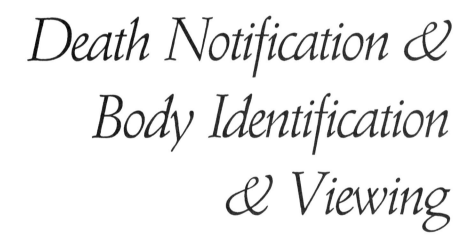

Death Notification &
Body Identification
& Viewing

Death notification is one of the most difficult tasks that a person may ever have to perform. While many people may never have to do a death notification with strangers, there is a high probability that they will have to do so within their own family or with friends. The way in which the death notification is done can have a significant impact upon the grief journey of the griever. While there are many elements involved within the death notification, it may be helpful to break it down into several components of the process.

Preparing to make the death notification
- Gathering the facts

- Assembling the notification team

- Defining individual roles & responsibilities

- Personal preparation

Making the notification
- Introductions & identification

- On-site considerations

- Making the notification

On-Scene support after the notification
- Preparing for and allowing for the reactions

- Protection for self and others

- Importance of presence

- Assessing and gathering their support system

- Answering the questions

- Practical assistance

- When to leave

Once you leave
- Self-care

- Taking it home

- Debriefing

- Follow-up

Death Notification Suggestions

Following a traumatic event, it is necessary to notify family members of the death of a loved one. Mental health personnel or clergy may be asked to serve on casualty / death notification teams. This document will serve as a guideline for this difficult task. It is expected that those making death notification will have sufficient experience and training to appropriately serve in this capacity.

Death Notification Procedure

1. The coroner or medical examiner is absolutely responsible for determining the identity of the deceased.

2. Notify in person. Don't call. Do not take any possessions of the victim to the notification. If there is absolutely no alternative to a phone call, arrange for a professional, neighbor, or a friend to be with the next of kin when the call comes.

3. Take someone with you (for example, an official who was at the scene, clergy, and someone who is experienced in dealing with shock and/or trained in CPR/medical emergency). Next of kin have been known to suffer heart attacks when notified. If a large group is to be notified, have a large team of notifiers.

4. Talk about your reactions to the death with your team member(s) before the notification to enable you to better focus on the family when you arrive.

5. Present credentials and ask to come in.

6. Sit down, ask them to sit down, and be sure you have the nearest next of kin (do not notify siblings before notifying parents or spouse). Never notify a child. Never use a child as a translator.

7. Use the victim's name... "Are you the parents of _____?"

8. Inform simply and directly with warmth and compassion.

9. Do not use expressions like "expired," "passed away," or "we've lost _____."

10. Sample script: "I'm afraid I have some very bad news for you." Pause a moment to allow them to "prepare." "Name has been involved in _____ and (s)he has died." Pause again. "I am so sorry that _____ died and you are having to face this." Adding your condolence is very important because it expresses feelings rather than facts, and invites them to express their own.

11. Understand that many thoughts are running through the minds of the person at this point. It is critical that the notification team to be prepared for any reaction including silence. A mistake commonly made is to fill the silence with empty words that are meaningless and irrelevant.

12. Continue to use the words "dead" or "died" through ongoing conversation. Continue to use the victim's name, not "body" or "the deceased."

13. Do not blame the victim in any way for what happened, even though he/she may have been fully or partially at fault.

14. Do not discount feelings, theirs or yours. Intense reactions are normal. Expect fight, flight, freezing, or other forms of regression. If someone goes into shock have them lie down, elevate their feet, keep them warm, monitor breathing and pulse, and call for medical assistance.

15. Join the survivors in their grief without being overwhelmed by it. Do not use clichés. Helpful remarks are simple, direct, validate, normalize, assure, empower, express concern. *Examples:* "I am so sorry for your loss." "It's harder than people think." "Most people who have gone through this react similarly to what you are experiencing." "If I were in your situation, I'd feel very _____ too."

16. Answer all questions honestly (requires knowing the facts before you go). Do not give more detail than is asked for, but be honest in your answers.

17. Offer to make calls, arrange for child care, call clergy, relatives, and employer. Provide them with a list of the calls you make as they will have difficulty remembering what you have told them.

18. When a child is killed and one parent is at home, notify that parent, then offer to take them to notify the other parent.

19. Do not speak to the media without the family's permission.

20. If identification of the body is necessary, transport next of kin to and from morgue and help prepare them by giving a physical description of the setting and the body.

21. Do not leave survivors alone. Arrange for someone to come and wait until they arrive before leaving.

22. When leaving let him/her or them know you will check back the next day to see how they are doing and if there is anything else you can do for them.

23. Call and visit again the next day. If the family does not want you to come, spend sometime on the phone and re-express willingness to answer all questions. They will probably have more questions than when they were first notified.

24. Ask the family if they are ready to receive "Name's" clothing, jewelry, etc. Honor their wishes. Possessions should be presented neatly in a box and not in a trash bag. Clothing should be dried thoroughly to eliminate bad odor. When the family receives the items, explain what the box contains and the condition of the items so they will know what to expect when they decide to open it.

25. If there is anything positive to say about the last moments, share them now. Give assurances such as "most people who are severely injured do not remember the direct assault and do not feel pain for some time." Do not say, "s(he) did not know what hit them" unless you are absolutely sure.

26. Let the survivor(s) know you care. The most beloved professionals and other first responders are those who are willing to share the pain of the loss. Attend the funeral if possible. This will mean a great deal to the family and reinforces a positive image of your profession.

27. Know exactly how to access immediate medical or mental health care should family members experience a crisis reaction that is beyond your response capability.

28. Debrief your own personal reactions with caring and qualified disaster mental health personnel on a frequent and regular basis - don't try to carry the emotional pain all by yourself, and don't let your emotions and the stress you naturally experience in empathizing with the bereaved build into a problem for you.

Source: This is adapted from curriculum on compassionate casualty and death notification for professional counselors and victim advocates, developed by Mothers Against Drunk Driving (MADD).
Reference: http://www.ncptsd.org/facts/disasters/fs_death_notification.html

Body Identification & Viewing

Caregivers may have to assist family members through the process of making an official body identification or viewing their loved one for the first time following a death. Caregivers can do a lot to help survivors through this difficult task that is critical to facing the reality of the death.

- Pre-observation of the body

- Gathering essential information

- Determining needs of the observer

- Supportive presence of others

- Preparing the observer

- Pacing

- Monitoring their reactions

- Supportive presence

- Privacy

- Follow-up

- Self-care & debriefing

Avoidance Phase Exercise

Consider the case study given to your group. You have been asked to provide a brief education to the family who is just starting into the avoidance phase. Your task is to help them prepare for what to expect. You will also talk with the three closest friends of the family who feel lost as to how they can help their grieving friends through their journey.

Your tasks

- Within your workgroup define the issues that the family is likely to face in the avoidance phase.

- What advice would you give the family?

- What advice would you give the friends as to how they can help in this phase?

- Break into pairs to play the role of caregiver and survivor. The caregiver will pretend that he/she is meeting with the survivor and his/her three best friends. You have already established rapport with the survivor and have spent time allowing them to ventilate and you have validated their grief and the loss. Now practice giving some brief education to help them prepare for what they can expect. Keep your advice simple and practical.

Notes:

SECTION VI

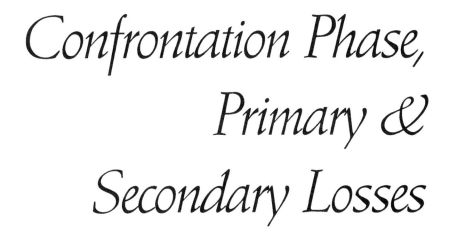

Confrontation Phase,
Primary &
Secondary Losses

Confrontation Phase

Reacting to the separation

• Dancing with the pain

• Struggling with the reality

• Internal issues: minimizing the loss; indifference

• External issues: possible changes in behavior

• Identification and mourning secondary losses

Primary and Secondary Losses
In your small groups, identify the primary and secondary losses that grieving people often face.

Primary Losses	Secondary Losses

Recollect and re-experience the deceased and the relationship

- Coming to terms with the reality of the relationship

- Reviving and re-experiencing the feelings

- Mourning and unloosing the ties and bonds with the deceased

Relinquishing the old attachments to the deceased and the old assumptive world

	Pre-trauma & Loss Assumptions	Post-trauma & Loss Revised Assumptions
Specific Assumptions		
Global Assumptions		

Primary needs disrupted after trauma

Considering your personal and professional experiences with trauma, grief and loss, identify what may change in these five core areas (Rosenbloom, Williams & Watkins, 1999; Pearlman & Saakvitne, 1995; McCann & Pearlman, 1990).

- Safety

- Trust

- Control

- Esteem

- Intimacy

Impact of Trauma on the Grief Process

In your small groups, consider the impact that trauma can have on the grief journey and identify how the trauma factors may impact the grief process.

Clinical Indicators of Complicated Mourning:

While it is not the task of most crisis response teams to evaluate the clinical indicators of complicated mourning, it is important for caregivers to be aware of some of the signs and symptoms that may indicate need for referral to higher systems of care. While many crisis response teams focus on intervention in the early aftermath of a critical incident or loss, provision of support through the long-term recovery journey is important.

"In brief, the demarcation between uncomplicated and complicated mourning is hazy at best and constantly changing. Such change is due not only to advancements in data collection in this area but also to the fact that no determination of abnormality can be made without taking into consideration the various sets of factors known to influence any response to loss. Reactions to loss can only be interpreted within the context of factors that circumscribe the particular loss for the particular mourner in the particular circumstances in which the loss took place" **Rando (1984.)**

Worden (1991) has described four classes of complicated grief:

Exaggerated grief:

Masked grief:

Chronic grief:

Delayed grief:

Rando (1993) lists some clinical indicators of complicated mourning:

1. A pattern of vulnerability to, sensitivity toward, or overreaction to experiences entailing loss and separation.

2. Psychological and behavioral restlessness, oversensitivity, arousal, over activity, geared up, constantly occupied, as if cessation of activity would permit surfacing of repressed anxiety provoking material.

3. Unusually high death anxiety focusing on self or loved ones.

4. Excessive and persistent over idealization of the deceased and/or unrealistic positive recollections of the relationship.

5. Rigid, compulsive, or ritualistic behavior sufficient to impinge on the mourner's freedom and well-being.

6. Persistent obsessive thoughts and preoccupation with the deceased and elements of the loss.

7. Inability to experience the various emotional reactions to loss typically found in the bereaved and/or uncharacteristically constricted affect.

8. Inability to articulate, within one's capacity existing feelings/thoughts about the loss/deceased.

9. Relationships with others are marked by fear of intimacy and other indices of avoidance stemming primarily form fear of future loss.

10. A pattern of self-destructive relationships commencing or escalating subsequent to the death, including compulsive caregiving and replacement relationships.

11. The commencement or escalation after the death of self-defeating, self-destructive, or acting-out behavior, including psychoactive substance dependence or abuse.

12. Chronic experiences of numbing, alienation, depersonalization, or other affects and occurrences that isolate the mourner from herself and others.

13. Chronic anger, annoyance or a combination of anger and depression (e.g. irritability, belligerence, intolerance).

Cost of Complicated Mourning

•Personal suffering

•Economic, social, political and philosophical, spiritual changes and adjustments

•Social networks

•Workplace

•Community

•Society as a whole – increased health insurance premiums, financial, and social costs of worker drug abuse, absenteeism, accidents, lowered productivity and product quality, and increased social violence.

Confrontation Phase Exercise

Consider the case study given to your group. You have been asked to provide a brief education to the family who is just starting into the confrontation phase. Your task is to help them prepare for what to expect. You will also talk with the three closest friends of the family who feel lost as to how they can help their grieving friends through their journey.

Your tasks

- Within your workgroup define the issues that the family is likely to face in the confrontation phase.

- What advice would you give the family?

- What advice would you give the friends as to how they can help in this phase?

- Break into pairs as caregiver and survivor. The caregiver will pretend that he/she is meeting with the survivor and his/her three best friends. Practice giving some brief education to help them prepare for what they can expect. Keep your advice simple and practical.

Notes:

SECTION VII

Accommodation Phase

Accommodation Phase

Readjust to move adaptively into the new world without forgetting the old.

- Moving and adapting

- Revision of life schema, assumptions

- Altering connections and relationships

- Fears of loosing and forgetting

- Guilt

- Forming a new existence in an altered world

Reinvesting
- Channeling energy in new endeavors

- Embracing the new and remembering the old

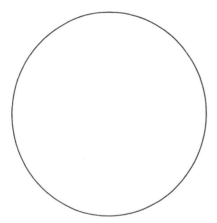

 **Co-Victim**

Survivor

Thriver

Accommodation Phase Exercise

Consider the case study given to your group. You have been asked to provide a brief education to the survivor who is just starting into the accommodation phase. Your task is to help them prepare for what to expect and help them rebuild their life. You will also talk with the three closest friends of the family who feel lost as to how they can help their grieving friends through their journey. The friends feel that their survivor friend is emotionally stuck and unable to rebuild his/her life.

Your tasks
- What questions would you ask the survivor?

- What advice would you give the friends as to how they can help in this phase?

- Break into pairs as caregiver and survivor. You will once again meet with the survivor and his/her three best friends. Practice providing some brief education to help them prepare for what they can expect and how they can help. Keep your advice simple and practical.

Helpful Techniques for Helping Survivors Rebuild Their Lives

Presence through the continuum

Connecting

Safety & control

Practical assistance with basic needs

Balancing "doing for" vs. "doing with"

Support network

Self-esteem & resiliency

Education & information

Life outside the grief and loss

Rituals & memorials beyond the funeral

Follow-up and follow through

From Trauma to Transformation

The experience of grief is painful and the process of mourning is difficult and complicated. However, sometimes we fail to recognize that there is sometimes a gift of personal growth and development that derives from the trauma or loss that survivors come to recognize. Helping survivors identify these positives is a critical part in helping put their lives back together and building personal hardiness to face new trauma and loss. Many survivors want to believe that something positive has come out of their pain. It also helps them to give back to others and can be a powerful part of their journey.

Reflection
List below some of the positives that you have discovered through this course through the video clips, class discussion and lecture, and self assessment of your own journey through trauma, loss, grief and mourning.

Notes:

SECTION VIII

Self-Care

Personal Impact on the Caregiver

Those who have a history of working with grieving people readily understand that there is a high cost of caring. Figley, (1995) notes that therapists who work with rape victims or other victims of crime may feel paranoid about their own safety and seek a greater security. He also indicates that, ironically, the most effective therapists are most vulnerable to this mirroring or contagion effect. He states, "Those who have enormous capacity for feeling and expressing empathy tend to be more at risk of compassion stress" (p.1). Thus, although the most effective caregivers enter the world of the suffering, this is not without a direct impact upon their own lives. Learning to give of oneself, and effectively conveying empathy while maintaining a healthy balance physically, emotionally and spiritually is not easily obtained or maintained. However, a failure to maintain this balance can result in premature burnout and a diminished capacity for compassionate and effective care.

Let us not underestimate how hard it is to be compassionate. Compassion is hard because it requires the inner disposition to go with others to the place where they are weak, vulnerable, lonely, and broken. But this is not our spontaneous response to suffering. What we desire most is to do away with suffering by fleeing from it or finding a quick cure of it. As busy, active, relevant ministers, we want to earn our bread by making a real contribution. This means first and foremost doing something to show that our presence makes a difference. And so we ignore our greatest gift, which is our ability to enter into solidarity with those who suffer (Henri Nouwen, 1991, p.34).

Reports by traumatized people indicate that family and friends discourage them from talking about their traumatic experiences after a few weeks because it is so distressing to the supporters (Figley, 1989). This is true not only of those who have directly experience the trauma, but also applies to those who have worked directly with those who have been traumatized. Upon return from intensive work with people in crisis, trauma and death, the crisis responder may feel a sense of isolation and lack of understanding of those around them.

Sometimes the trauma that was witnessed in the lives of those victimized is too horrific and too personal for the crisis responder to share with those closest to them for fear of exposing them to the traumatizing experiences. At other times, family and friends lack an understanding of the nature and impact of the crisis work on their loved one and fail to understand the interpersonal impact that crisis work can have on their loved one. While loved ones may provide a listening ear, more often than not, they will need some education regarding how they can best help the crisis responder. Thus it is essential for crisis responders to have an appropriate outlet to process the events that they have experienced. This is often best accomplished by someone other than one's family. Frequently, the best person to process with is another crisis responder or a mental health provider who is trained in crisis response. Processing the crisis response deployment with the team members who also served on the incident can be extremely beneficial. There is a bond that responders share when they have experienced difficulty in the same situation. In these relationships there is an understanding that others will never experience and much can be said without words.

Concepts for Self-Care

Emotional exhaustion appears to be the key factor that that is looked at in assessment tools used to measure levels of burnout and in most descriptions and definitions of burnout.

According to Pines and Aronson (1988), burnout is a "state of physical, emotional, and mental exhaustion caused by a long term involvement in emotionally demanding situations" (p.9). Burnout is a process (rather then a fixed condition) that begins gradually and becomes progressively worse (Cherniss, 1980; Maslach, 1976, 1982). The process of burnout includes (a) gradual exposure to job strain (Courage & Williams, 1986), (b) erosion of idealism (Freudenberger, 1986; Pines, Aronson, & Kafry, 1981), and (c) a void of achievement (Pines & Maslach, 1980). There is also an accumulation of intense contact with clients (Maslach & Jackson, 1981).

Multiple studies have documented that exposure to the injured and dying is highly stressful and has significant negative effects on mental health (Beaton & Murphy, 1993). Thus, it is essential that one identify those stressors that are more likely to have a negative impact on disaster workers and provide appropriate care to help mitigate the impact. In a comprehensive review of the empirical research on the symptoms of burnout, Kahill (1988) identified five categories of symptoms.

1. Physical symptoms
2. Emotional syptoms
3. Behavioral symptoms
4. Work-related symptoms
5. Interpersonal symptoms

The research points to a number of indicators of secondary traumatic stress that may result from trauma work. Some of these indicators may include

1. Distressing emotions (Courtois, 1988; McCann & Pearlman, 1990; Scurfield, 1985), including sadness or grief, depression, anxiety, dread and horror, fear, rage, or shame.

2. Intrusive imagery by the trauma worker of the client's traumatic material (Courtois, 1988; Herman, 1992; McCann & Pearlman, 1990), such as nightmares, flooding, and flashbacks of images generated during and following the client's recounting of traumatic events.

3. Numbing or avoidance of efforts to elicit or work with traumatic material from the client, including dissociation (Courtois, 1988; Herman, 1992; McCann & Pearlman, 1990; McCann & Pearlman, 1990; Silver, 1986).

4. Somatic complaints (Figley, 1986; Herman, 1992) including sleep difficulty, headaches, gastrointestinal distress, and heart palpitations.

5. Addictive or compulsive behaviors, including substance abuse, workaholism (Boylin & Briggie, 1987), and compulsive eating.

6. Physiological arousal (McCann & Pearlman, 1990; Van der Kolk, 1987).

7. Impairment of day-to-day functioning in social and personal roles, such as missed or canceled appointments; decreased use of supervision or cotherapy (Boylin & Briggie, 1987); chronic lateness; a decreased ability to engage in self-care behaviors, including personal therapy; and feelings of isolation, alienation, or lack of appreciation (Boylin & Briggie, 1987).

In the recent years, there has been a significant amount of research and writing on issues relating to compassion fatigue. Figley (2002, p.7) gives an excellent portrayal of common compassion fatigue burnout symptoms as reflected in the following chart.

Examples of Compassion Fatigue Burnout Symptoms	
Cognitive	Lowered concentration Decreased self-esteem Apathy Rigidity Disorientation Perfectionism Minimization Preoccupation with trauma Thoughts of self-harm or harm to others
Emotional	Powerlessness Anxiety Guilt Anger/rage Survivor guilt Shutdown Numbness Fear Helplessness Sadness Depression Emotional rollercoaster Depleted Overly sensitive
Behavioral	Impatient Irritable Withdrawn Moody Regression Sleep disturbance Nightmares Appetite changes Hypervigilance Elevated startle response Accident proneness Losing things

Spiritual	Questioning the meaning of life Loss of purpose Lack of self-satisfaction Pervasive hopelessness Anger at God Questioning prior religious beliefs Loss of faith in a higher power Greater skepticism about religion
Personal Relations	Withdrawal Decreased interest in intimacy or sex Mistrust Isolation from others Overprotection as a parent Projection of anger or blame Intolerance Loneliness Increased interpersonal conflicts
Somatic	Shock Sweating Rapid heartbeat Breathing difficulties Aches and pains Dizziness Increased number and intensity of medical maladies Impaired immune system Other somatic complaints
Work Performance	Low morale Low motivation Avoiding tasks Obsession about details Apathy Negativity Lack of appreciation Detachment Poor work commitments Staff conflicts Absenteeism Exhaustion Irritability Withdrawal from colleagues

When people are exposed to primary stressors and exhibit a certain set of symptoms, it is referred to as "post traumatic stress disorder (PTSD)." When a person is exposed to secondary stressors and experiencing a set of symptoms, it is referred to as "secondary traumatic stress disorder (STSD)." The following chart depicts and contracts the symptoms of PTSD with STSD.

Suggested Distinctions between the Diagnostic Criteria for Primary and Secondary Traumatic Stress Disorder.
(Figley, 1995, p. 8).

Primary	Secondary

A. Stressor:
Experienced an event outside the range of usual human experiences that would be markedly distressing to almost anyone; an event such as
  1. Serious threat to self
  2. Sudden destruction of one's environs
	A. Stressor:
	Experienced an event outside the range of usual human experiences that would be markedly distressing to almost anyone; an event such as:
	1. Serious threat to traumatized person
	2. Sudden destruction of TP's environs

B. Reexperiencing Trauma Event 1. Recollections of event 2. Dreams of event 3. Sudden reexperiencing of event 4. Distress of reminders of event	B. Reexperiencing Trauma Event 1. Recollections of event/TP 2. Dreams of event/TP 3. Sudden reexperiencing of event/TP 4. Reminders of TP/ event distressing
C. Avoidance/Numbing of Reminders 1. Efforts to avoid thoughts/feelings 2. Efforts to avoid activities/situations 3. Psychogenic amnesia 4. Diminished interest in activities 5. Detachment/estrangements from others 6. Diminished affect 7. Sense of foreshortened future	C. Avoidance/Numbing of Reminders 1. Efforts to avoid thoughts/feelings 2. Efforts to avoid activities/situations 3. Psychogenic amnesia 4. Diminished interest in activities 5. Detachment/estrangements from others 6. Diminished affect 7. Sense of foreshortened future
D. Persistent Arousal 1. Difficulty falling/staying asleep 2. Irritability or outbursts of anger 3. Difficulty concentrating 4. Hypervigilance for self 5. Exaggerated startle response 6. Physiologic reactivity to cues	D. Persistent Arousal 1. Difficulty falling/staying asleep 2. Irritability or outbursts of anger 3. Difficulty concentrating 4. Hypervigilance for TP 5. Exaggerated startle response 6. Physiologic reactivity to cues
(Symptoms under one month duration are considered normal, acute, crisis-related reactions. Those not manifesting symptoms until six months or more following the event are delayed PTSD or STSD.)	

Personal Signs and Symptoms Exercise

Discuss with your partner your personal indicators and symptoms of excessive stress and burnout.

Self-Care and Renewal Concepts

Define how you refuel in the following areas:

Physically

Psychologically

Emotionally

Spiritually

DROP-IT

A post-deployment out-processing model for
emergency services personnel, crisis and disaster relief workers
(Ellers, K. L., 2005)

Providing care for disaster and trauma survivors can have a powerful and lasting impact upon caregivers. These deployments have potential to create a life altering long-term impact in one's life. These impacts can be positive and/or negative. While many factors play into the impact of the deployment upon one's life, exposure to the traumatic stories and victims may lead to vicarious traumatization, compassion fatigue and burnout. It is critical that caregivers have an opportunity to process from the deployment before reintegration back into their home and normal environments and develop a plan for reintegration and ongoing care as needed. The DROP-IT model for out-processing of caregivers provides a simple six step process that will facilitate recounting the story; processing the experiences, thoughts and feelings associated with the deployment; assessment; preparation and education for post assignment reactions; and developing a plan for transitioning into normal life. This model is specifically designed to facilitate reentry from intensive deployments relating to mass casualty, DMORT, death notifications, and working with trauma survivors. While it is recommended that the DROP-IT out-processing intervention be done one-on-one in a face-to-face interview, if this is not possible, it can also be done by phone. The DROP-IT Model should be considered as one of many tools available within the broad range of Critical Incident Stress Management Interventions.

D   <u>Describe</u> their role and duties in the deployment.

R   <u>Recall</u> significant experiences, images thoughts and feelings.

O   <u>Orientation</u> to present status through self-assessment.

P   <u>Predict</u> and prepare for post-deployment challenges.

I   <u>Identify</u> the most difficult and positive elements of the deployment.

T   <u>Transition</u> plan for reintegration, self-care, and follow-up.

While the model remains the same, the prompting questions which have been given should be adapted to each situation as necessary.

Introduction:
The facilitator should take time to engage the person and explain the goals and process of the out-processing session. The session should be structured in a professional but casual manner and should avoid a clinical feel to the interview.

D   <u>Describe</u> **their role in the deployment.**

This introductory component is non-threatening and cognitive-based point of entry into the DROP-IT Model. People generally like to tell their story and this provides an opportunity for them to process their role and the accompanying details of their assignment. The attentive, active listening and engaging presence of the facilitator sets the stage for how the rest of the interview will go.

R   <u>Recall</u> **significant experiences, images, thoughts and feelings.**

This component encourages a balance of both cognitive and affective processes to facilitate the integration of thoughts, feelings, and images which may have not been acknowledged during active deployment. This component facilitates confirmation of the reality of the experience as the person gives voice to their experience and is acknowledged by the caregiver.

O   <u>Orientation</u> **to present status through self-assessment.**

This component starts by taking a personal inventory, doing an impact assessment, identifying stressors and resources, and assessing self-perception of coping. The goal is to promote self-assessment and processing their self-perception of coping.

P   <u>Predict</u> **and prepare for post-deployment challenges.**

This component facilitates looking at past deployments or similar experiences and identifying effective coping mechanisms. It also allows for consideration of post-deployment factors which may positively or negatively impact them. Summarizing key points to create awareness which may be helpful in building personal hardiness and resiliency.

I   <u>Identify</u> **difficult and positive elements of the deployment.**

This component helps the person to summarize and give voice to the most difficult elements of the deployment. Moving to the positive elements of the assignment may help counter negative experiences of the deployment

T   <u>Transition</u> **plan for reintegration and follow-up.**

This last component helps the person assess their need for post-deployment follow-up care and identify a plan for reintegration. Helping the person identify self-care activities and support systems are useful. Giving information for follow-up care or arranging for a follow-up contact can also be helpful. Briefly highlighting the reentry issues and effective reentry concepts may be helpful.

Upon completion of this out-processing intervention, it is recommended that several minutes be set aside for quiet reflection or utilization of a visualization exercise to process remaining thoughts, feelings and images. It may also be helpful to teach basic self-care and self-soothing techniques to enhance coping with ongoing post-deployment residual carryover of post deployment issues.

References

Amick-McMullan, A., Kilpatrick, D., Veronen, L., and Smith, S. (1989). Family survivors of homicide victims; Theoretical perspectives and an exploratory study. *Journal of Traumatic Stress, 2(1), 21-35.*

Beaton, R., & Murphy, S.A. (1993). Sources of occupational stress among firefighters/EMSs and firefighter/paramedics and correlations with job-related outcomes. *Prehospital and Disaster Medicine,* 8, 140-150.

Boylin, W. M., & Briggie, C. R. (1987). The Healthy therapist: The contribution of symbolic-experiential family therapy. *Family Therapy, 14* (30), 247-256.

Bradach, K. & Jordan, J. (1995). Long-term effects of a family history of traumatic death on adolescent individuation. *Death Studies 19, 315-326.*

Breslau, N., Daivs, G.C., Andreski, P.L, & Peterson, E, (1991). Traumatic events and posttraumatic stress disorder in urban populations of young adults. *Achieves of General Psychiatry*, 48(3), 216-222.

Centers for Disease Control. (2002). Morbidity and Mortality Weekly Report.

Cherniss, C. (1980). *Staff burnout: Job stress in the human services.* Beverly Hills, Calif.: Sage.

Courage, M.M., & Williams, D.M. (1986). *An approach to the study of burnout in professional care providers in human service organizations.* Journal of Social Service Research, *10(1), 7-22.*

Courtois, C. (1988). *Healing the incest wound: Adult survivors in therapy.* New York: Norton.

Ditchick, F. (1990). *The reactions of husbands and wives to the death of their child and its effect on their marital relationship.* Adephui University: Unpublished dissertation.

Doka, K. (1989). *Disenfranchised Grief: Recognizing Hidden Sorrow.* Lanham, MD: Lexington Books.

Duffy, J.D., (1997). The Neural Substrates of Emotion. *Psychiatric Annals,* January 1997.

Dyregrov, A., Solomon, R., & Bassoe, C.F. (2000). Mental mobilization processes in critical incident stress situations. *International Journal of Emergency Mental Health,* Spring: 2(2): 73-81.

Elliott, D.M. (1997). Traumatic events: prevalence and delayed recall in the general population. *Journal of Consulting and Clinical Psychology,* 65(8), 811-820.

Everly, G.S., & Mitchell, J.T. (2003). *Critical Incident Stress Management: Individual Crisis Intervention and Peer Support.* Ellicott City, MD: International Critical Incident Stress Foundation.

Figley, C.R. (2002). *Treating Compassion Fatigue.* New York: Brunner-Routlidge.

Figley, C.R. (1996, December). Integrating the theoretical and clinical components of grief and PTSD. Trauma and Loss [Workshop]. Toronto: Trauma and Loss Seminar.

Figley, C. R. (Ed.). (1995). *Compassion fatigue: Coping with secondary traumatic stress disorder in those who treat the traumatized.* New York: Brunner/Mazel.

Figley, C. R., & Kleber, R. J. (1995). Beyond the "victim": Secondary traumatic stress. In R. J. Kebler, C. R. Figley, & B. P. R. Gersons (Eds.). *Beyond Trauma: Cultural and Societal Dynamics* (pp. 75-98). New York: Plenum.

Figley, C. R. (1989). *Helping Traumatized Families.* SFO: Jossey-Bass.

Figley, C.R. (1986). *Traumatic stress: The role of the family and social support system. In C.R. Figley, (Ed.), Trauma and its wake: Vol. 2. Trumatic stress theory, research, and intervention (pp. 39-54). New York:B runner/Mazel.*

Figley, C.R. (1983). Catastrophes: Any overview of family reactions. In C.R. Figley & H.I. McCubbin (Eds.), *Stress and the family: Vol. 2. Coping with catastrophe,* New York: Brunner/Mazel. *(pp. 3-20).*

Friedman, M. J. (2000). PTSD diagnosis and treatment for mental health clinicians. In M.Scott & J. Palmer (Eds.). *Trauma and post-traumatic stress disorder* (pp. 1-14) New York: Cassell.

Freudenberger, H. J. (1986). The issues of staff burnout in therapeutic communities. *Journal of Psychoactive Drugs, 18* (2), 247-251.

Gallup, G.G., & Maser, J.D. (1977). Tonic immobility: Evolutionary underpinnings of human catalepsy and catatonia. In M.E. P. Seligman & J.D. Maser (Eds.), *Psychopathology: Experimental models* (pp. 334-357). San Francisco: W.H. Freeman.

Gentry, E. J., Baranowsky, A. B., and Dunning, K. (2002). ARP: The accelerated recovery program (ARP) for compassion fatigue. In C. R. Figley (Ed.). *Treating Compassion Fatigue.* New York: Brunner-Routledge.

Goleman, D. (1998). *Working with Emotional Intelligence.* New York: Bantam Books.

Herman, J. L. (1992). Complex PTSD: A syndrome in survivors of prolonged and repeated trauma. *Journal of Traumatic Stress,* 5 (3), 377-391.

Herman, J. L. (1997). *Trauma and Recovery: The aftermath of violence B from domestic abuse to political terror.* New York: Basic Books.

Iserson, Kenneth V., M.D., (1999). *Grave Words: Notifying Survivors about Sudden, Unexpected Deaths*. Tucson, AZ: Galen Press, Ltd.

Kahill, S. (1988). Interventions for burnout in the helping professions: A review of the empirical evidence. *Canadian Journal of Counseling Review, 22* (3), 310-342.

Kulka, R.A., Schlenger, W.E., Fairbank. J.A., Hough, R.L., Jordan, B.K., Marmar, C.R., & Weiss, D.S., (1990). Trauma and the Vietnam war generation: Report of findings from the National Vietnam Veterans Readjustment Study. New York: Brunner/Mazel.

Landry, L. P. (1999). Secondary traumatic stress disorder in the therapists from the Oklahoma City bombing [Dissertation]. University of North Texas (UMI No. AAT99-81105).

Leash, R. Moroni, LCSW, MSHCA. *Death Notification: A Practical Guide to the Process*. Hinesburg, VT: Upper Access, Inc.

LeDoux, J. (1996). *The Emotional Brain*. New York: Basic Books.

Lehman, D., and Wortman, C. (1987). Long-term effects of losing a spouse or child in a motor vehicle crash. *Journal of Personality and Social Psychology, 52(1), 218-231.*

Lindy, J. (1985). The trauma membrane and other clinical concepts derived from psychotherapeutic work with survivors of natural disasters. *Psychiatric Annals, 15(3), 153-160.*

Martin, T.L. & Doka, K.J. (2000). *Men Don't Cry...Women Do: Transcending Gender Stereotypes of Grief*. Philadelpia, PA: Brunner/Mazel

Maslach C. (1982). *The burnout: The cost of caring*. Englewood Cliffs, NJ: Prentice-Hall.

Maslach, C., & Jackson, S. E. (1981). The measurement of experienced burnout. *Journal of Occupational Behavior, 2* (2), 99-113.

Maslach C. (1976). Burn-out. *Human Behavior, 5* (9), 16-22.

McCann, I. L., & Pealman, L.A. (1990). *Psychological Trauma and the Adult Survivor*. New York: Brunner/Mazel.

Mercer, D. (1993, October). Drunk driving victimization or non-victimization effects on volunteer victim advocates. *Paper presented at the International Society of Traumatic Stress Studies, San Antonio, TX.*

Mitchell, K.R., & Anderson, H. (1983). *All Our Losses all Our Griefs*. Louisville: Westminster John Knox Press.

Nader, K.O. (2002) Childhood traumatic loss: the interaction of trauma and grief. In C.R. Figley (Ed.). *Death and Trauma: The Traumatology of Grieving.* Washington, D.C: Taylor & Francis.

Nouwen, H. J. (1991). *The Way of the Heart: Desert Spirituality and Contemporary Ministry.* San Francisco: Harper San Francisco.

Parkes, C. (1981). Emotional involvement of the family during the period preceding death. In *Acute Grief* (Eds.) Margolis, O,, Raether, H., Kutscher, A., Power, B., Seeland, I., DeBellis, R., and Cheno, D. New York: Columbia Press.

Parkes, C.M. (1988). Bereavement as a psychosocial transition: Processes of adaptation to change. *Journal of Social Issues, 11(3), 53-65.*

Pearlman, L.A., & Saakvitne, K.W. (1995). *Trauma and the Therapist: Countertransference and Vicarious Traumatization with Incest Survivors.* New York: W.W. Norton.

Perry, B.D., Pollard, R.A., Blakey, T.L., Baker, W.L., &Vigilante, D. (1995). Childhood trauma, the neurobiology of adaptation, and "use-dependent" development of the brain: How "states" become "traits." *Infant Mental Health Journal,* 16(4), 271-291.

Pines, A., Aronson, E., & Kafry, D. (1981). *Burnout: From tedium to personal growth.* New York: Free Press.

Pines, A., & Maslach, C. (1980). Combating staff burnout in child care centers: a case study. *Child Care Quarterly, 9,* 5-16

Rando, T. A. (1993). *Treatment of Complicated Mourning.* Champaign, IL: Research Press.

Rando, T.A. (1984). *Grief, dying and death: Clinical interventions for caregivers.* Champaign, IL: Research Press.

Raphael, B. (1983). *The anatomy of bereavement.* New York: Basic.

Redmond, L. (1989). *Surviving: When someone you love was murdered.* Clearwater, FL: Psychological Consultation and Education Services.

Rinear, E.E. (1988). Psychosocial aspects of parental response patterns to the death of a child by homicide. *Journal of Traumatic Stress, 1(3), 305-322.*

Rosenblooom, D., Williams, M.B., & Watkins, B.E. (1999). *Life After Trauma: A Workbook for Healing.* New York: Guilford Press.

Rynearson, E.K., & McCreery, J.M. (1993). Bereavement after homicide: A synergism of trauma and loss. *American Journal of Psychiatry, 150(2), 258-261.*

Schanfield, S., Swain, B., & Benjamin, G. (1987). Parents' resonses to the death of adult children from accidents and cancer: A comparison. *Omega, 17, 289-297.*

Scurfield, R. M. (1985). Post-trauma stress assessment and treatment: Overview and formulations. In C.R. Figley (Ed.). *Trauma and its wake: The study and treatment of post-traumatic stress disorder* (pp. 219-256). New York: Brunner/Mazel.

Sherman, S. (1994). Leaders Learn to Heed the Voice Within. *Fortune*, August 22, 1994.

Silver, S. M. (1986). An impatient program for post-traumatic stress disorder: Context and treatment. In C. R. Figley (Ed.). *Trauma and its wake: Vol. 2. Traumatic stress theory, research, and intervention* (pp. 213-231). New York: Brunner/Mazel

Spungen, D. (1999). *Traumatic Grief: The Synergism of Trauma and Grief.* From a train-the-trainer Traumatic Grief Symposium Series.

Stamm, B. H. (Ed.). (1995). *Secondary traumatic stress: Self-care issues for clinicians, researchers, and educators.* Lutherville, MD: Sidran Press.

Steele, L. (1992). Risk factor profile for bereaved spouses. *Death Studies,* 16(5, September-October, 387-399.

Strobe, W., Strobe, M. & Domittner, G. (1988). Individual and situational differences in recovery from bereavement: A risk group identified. *Journal of Social Issues, 44(3), 143-158).*

Van der Kolk, B. (1987). *Psychological Trauma.* Washington, DC: American Psychiatric Press.

Vogel, G. (1997). Scientists Probe Feelings Behind Decision Making. *Science,* February 28, 1997.

Weiss, R., et al. (1986). Widowers as a contrasting group. *The First Year of Bereavement.* New York: John Wiley and Sons.

Weiss, R. (1988). *Recovery from bereavement: Findings and issues in preventing mental disorders.* Washington, DC: National Institute of Mental Health, 108-121.

Wolvin, A. &; Coakley, C, (1982). Listening. Dubuque, Iowa: Wm. C. Brown Publishers.

Worden, J. W. (1982). *Grief counseling and grief therapy: A handbook for the mental health practitioners.* New York: Springer.

Wright, H.N. (2003). *The New Guide to Crisis and Trauma Counseling: A Practical Guide for Ministers, Counselors and Lay Counselors.* Ventura, CA: Regal.

Grief Following Trauma
Resource Page

Websites

American Academy of Bereavement: www.bereavementacademy.com

American Association of Suicidology: www.suicdiology.org

American Foundation for Suicide Prevention: www.afsp.org

Anxiety Disorders Association of America: www.adaa.org

Aquarius Health Care Videos: www.aquariusproductions.com

Association for Death Education and Counseling: www.adec.org

Association of Traumatic Stress Specialists: www.atss-hq.com

Bereavement Magazine: www.bereavementmag.com

Candlelighters Child Loss: www.candlelighters.org

CDC – National Center for Injury Prevention and Control: www.cdc.gov/ncipc

Centering Corporation: www.centering.org

Center for Loss: www.centerforloss.com

Chevron Publishing: www.chevronpublishing.com

International Society for Traumatic Stress Studies: www.istss.org

Family Source: www.family-source.com

Genesis Bereavement Resources: www.genesis-resources.com

MADD – Mothers Against Drunk Drivers: www.madd.org

National Alliance for the Mentally Ill: www.nami.org

National Center for PTSD: www.ncptsd.org

National Child Traumatic Stress Network: www.nctsnet.org

National Mental Health Association: www.nmha.org

NIMH – National Institute of Mental Health: www.nimh.nih.gov

Office for Victims of Crime Resources: www.ojpusdoj.gov/ovc

Parents of Murdered Children: www.pomc.com

Parents of Suicide Support: www.parentsofsuicide.com

PTSD Alliance: www.ptsdalliance.com

SAMHSA – Substance Abuse/Mental Health Services: www.samhsa.gov

SHARE Infant Loss: www.nationalshareoffice.com

Sidran Traumatic Stress Foundation: www.sidran.org

SIDS – Sudden Infant Death Syndrome: www.sids.org

Suicide Information Education Center: www.siec.ca

Widowed Persons Service: www.aolmember.aarp.org

Printed Resources

Manning, Doug. (1979). *Don't take My Grief Away from Me.* Oklahoma City, OK: In-Sight Books, Inc.

Hewett, John H. (1980). *After Suicide.* Philadelphia, PA: Westminster Press

Rando, T.A. (1984). *Grief, Dying and Death: Clinical Interventions for Caregivers.* Champaign, IL: Research Press

Rando, T.A. (1986). *Parental Loss of a Child.* Champaign, IL: Research Press

Rando, T.A. (1993). *Treatment of Complicated Mourning.* Champaign, IL: Research Press.

Schiff, Harriet Sarnoff, (1977). *The Bereaved Parent.* New York, NY: Crown Publishers.

Worden, J.W. (1982). *Grief counseling and Grief Therapy: A Handbook for the Mental Health Practitioner.* New York, NY: Springer.

Worden, J.W. (2001) *Children and Grief: When a Parent Dies.* New York, NY: Guilford Press.

Videos/DVDs

PTSD: Understanding Post Traumatic Stress Disorder
PTSD Alliance
450 West 15th Street, 7th Floor
New York, NY 10011
1-877-507-PTSD

Strong At The Broken Places: Turning Trauma into Recovery
Cambridge Documentary Films, Inc.
www.cambridgedocumentaryfilms.org
617-484-3993

Tear Soup: A Recipe for Healing After Loss
Grief Watch
www.griefwatch.com

Victims Speak Out: Help, Hope, and Healing
Office for Victims of Crime
800-627-6872

When Helping Hurts: Sustaining Trauma Workers
Gift From Within
16 Cobb Hill Road
Camden, Maine 04843
207-236-8858

Appendix

End of Day Reflection Exercise

Take several minutes to reflect on the following questions and discuss them with the person next to you before leaving.

Of the content covered today, what has impacted me the most is…

Regarding grief and trauma, I have been thinking…

Right now I feel…

What is the one thing that makes you laugh?

How to Know You Need Help

When a loved one dies, the survivor's world turns upside down. Nothing seems the same because nothing is the same. The grieving process creates a new "normal." During this process, many grieving people question their sanity. They have never felt the intense physical and emotional pain or the depth of sadness and depression that they are now experiencing.

Grief is emotionally and physically painful, but given time and support, most people work through it in a healthy way. A person's grief may be more complicated or difficult if ...

> ... the relationship one had with the deceased was ambivalent or angry.
> ... the person has experienced many deaths over a short period of time.
> ... the death was unexpected, sudden or violent.
> ... the body was not viewed.
> ... prior mental or physical illness existed.
> ... the death was witnessed by the grieving person.
> ... adequate support was not given.

These particular circumstances may cause the grieving person to feel something is wrong with him or her or that he or she needs additional assistance. Even without these specific circumstances, however, some people may still experience difficult grief.

Be aware that most people will experience most of these symptoms for a short time. When grief is intense and shows no sign? of lessening, it may be helpful to find someone who can help during these difficult times.

Should you Consult a Professional Counselor?

✦The greatest indication of needing additional assistance comes from your own sense of need. Do you   feel like something is wrong or that you are "going crazy?"

✦It is important to be able to express yourself in words or actions. Do you feel you are suppressing your grief because you cannot speak about it?

✦Are you assuming the role of caregiver for the rest of the family? Do you put your grief on hold so you can take care of others? Is this additional responsibility making you angry or resentful?

✦Grief is painful and most of us have difficulty coping with painful thoughts and feelings. Are you trying to find relief by drinking alcohol or taking more prescription or over-the-counter drugs? Are you engaging in risky behaviors such as speeding or reckless driving? Are you having thoughts of harming yourself or others?

✦It hurts to lose someone you love. Sometimes we feel we do not want to get close to anyone again because we might lose him or her, too. Does this pervasive fear prevent you from getting too close to anyone?

✦It helps to find things to keep us busy when we are grieving as long as it doesn't become a way of avoiding grief. Everyone needs a respite from grief; however, running away from your grief is unhealthy. Do you feel that you are keeping busier than usual?

> ✦ After a death, it is normal for our thoughts to be focused almost entirely on the deceased. If you are constantly preoccupied or experience incessant thoughts of the death over long periods, however, you may need to seek some help.

How to Say "I'm Sorry" to Those Who Grieve

Offering condolences and comfort to grieving people is difficult for most of us. We are at a loss as to what to say or do. Too often, we shy away because we do not feel comfortable saying anything or we are afraid we will cause them additional sadness.

One thing to remember is that talking about the loved one who died is not going to make grieving people remember their loss or feel sad. Those memories are already there. If grieving people cry or show other emotions, you are not the cause. Understand that strong emotions are a normal part of the grieving process. Most grieving people want to talk about their loved one and enjoy hearing stories you have to tell.

Many of us want to offer comfort and great compassion to those who have lost a loved one. Not knowing what to say or fear of saying the wrong thing keeps us from reaching out to others in need. We recognize when someone is hurting and we fear adding to that hurt by saying or doing something that might be taken the wrong way. We often are afraid of strong emotions and feel unequipped to handle them. Sometimes, the death of someone reminds us of our own mortality and we do not want to be saddened.

"Condoling actions reaffirm our bonds to humanity; they strengthen and enlarge each of us. Each word of comfort, each letter of condolence, each act of helpful service has the potential to serve not only as a message of sympathy, but as a song of compassion and truth."

Offering Condolences

✦Take time to learn something about the grieving process. Most people think grief should end as soon as the funeral service is over. Grieving is a long and difficult path. It is an emotional, physical, spiritual and social reaction.

✦Many factors will determine the depth of someone's grief. Grief never ends. Many times, memories will remind people that their loved one is no longer with them. Their grief will lessen but will never disappear.

✦Do not offer advice even if you have experienced a similar loss. Instead, offer suggestions. Remember that your grief is different and the things that helped you may not always help someone else.

✦Keep your words simple. "I'm so sorry for your loss," can say it all.

✦Sometimes words are not enough. At these times, a hug or holding the person's hand can convey concern and sympathy.

✦Remember that nothing you can say or do will take away a person's grief. You cannot "fix" someone, make him or her happy or return him or her to the way he or she was before the death.
If you want to write your condolences, do not put it off. You are more likely to say what you want to say and convey your sincerity more effectively if you do it immediately.

✦Be sincere.

✦Do not say, "I know what you're going through." You do not.

✦Always mention the deceased by name.

✦Do not offer assistance unless you are prepared to follow through with actions.

Nancy Crump, D.W. Newcomer's Sons

Surviving a Sudden Death

More than any other factor, the unexpected, sudden death of a loved one determines the course of your grief. This abrupt death contributes to your complex feelings.

Sudden death can result from accidents, suicides, homicides and disasters. A death from a heart attack or stroke can also be considered a sudden death. Essentially, a sudden death is any death for which we have no time to prepare.

Unlike other deaths, sudden death has the potential of throwing you into a world that seems out of control. At one level, you know your loved one has died. You can talk about it and relive past events. At another level, the death is unbelievable — you expect your loved one to come walking through the door at any minute. The death occurs without warning, leaving you with no way to adapt and use the coping skills you need. You are overwhelmed, bewildered, anxious and fearful.

One of the most pervasive feelings following a sudden death is the sense that the world is no longer a safe and predictable place. You may have an overwhelming sense that someone else you love will die. It may cause you to become hyper-vigilant, watching for danger so you can protect your loved ones or yourself. It may also cause problems in your relationships with others.

The intensity of the emotions and the prolonged period of acute grief may leave you feeling as if you are "going crazy." You have probably never had any experience like this. You are not alone if you feel you are not equipped to deal with the concerns and issues that develop from this type of death.

Common Reactions to a Sudden Death

✦You feel a high level of distress with a lowered capacity to cope.
✦Your feelings of control and security may dwindle. You may abandon your assumptions and expectations about life.
✦You may have a sense of unfinished business because you were unable to say goodbye.
✦You may experience acute grief, shock and numbness for a prolonged time.
✦You may find that you need to reconstruct the events leading to the death.
✦The intensity of your emotions may increase.

Your Emotional and Physical Well Being

✦Rest, exercise and eat properly.
✦Try to maintain your daily routines and schedule.
✦Express your pain to someone, such as a trusted friend or counselor, who will understand and acknowledge your feelings.
✦Be honest about all of your feelings and questions.
✦Join a support group. Check with area hospitals or churches for groups.
✦Allow yourself to feel your grief and express your emotions.
✦Build up your spiritual resources daily with nature walks, poetry, prayer partners, inspirational reading or worship services.
✦Try to forgive others for being insensitive.
✦Seek out others who knew your loved one and let them share their stories.
✦Take a break from your grief. It is healthy for you to do something that makes you feel better.

Nancy Crump, D.W. Newcomer's Sons

TIPS FOR FAMILIES EXPERIENCING TRAUMATIC DEATH

When death comes suddenly, unexpectedly, and violently, family members are often left in a state of shock and numbness. They are often unable to think clearly and react decisively. Listed below are some guidelines to assist families in the weeks and months ahead.

1.   **As soon as possible, identify your closest "inner circle" of family and friends.** Who do you trust and feel you can depend upon? Of these, identify who will be there to listen to you when you need to talk, help with the funeral arrangements, organize food and chores, and be a spokesperson for the family.

2.   **Family and friends will want to help, but may need direction about what is "helpful" to you.** Let people know your limits - what you want done for you, and how much.

3.   **Immediately after the notification of the death, select one person to make telephone calls to notify others of the death.** Remember that there may be some people who need to be notified in person rather than by telephone.

4.   **If the death of your loved one is considered "high profile," you may be contacted by the media.** You may want to select someone in your support system to deal with the media. Consider carefully how you want to deal with their questions, if at all. Decide whether or not you want to watch the news coverage of the death of your loved one. You may want someone to tape the news stories so you can watch them later.

5.   **Remember that nothing affects you emotionally that doesn't also affect you physically.** You have no choice about this death happening, but you do have a choice about how you take care of yourself. Do those things you know are good for you.

> ✦   Get as much rest as possible. Lie down and close your eyes even if you can't sleep.

> ✦   Eat something small several times a day rather than trying to sit down to a large meal three times a day.

> ✦   Get out of the house and away from people, telephone calls, and memories for a while. Make sure you take someone with you, especially if you drive. If you do drive, remember that it is normal to become confused and disoriented, so pay close attention to your driving.

> ✦   Get a physical check-sip as soon as possible. If possible avoid taking medications to cover your grief. It will only prolong dealing with your emotions.

---

6. **Take a close friend or family member when making funeral arrangement.** Limit the number of people you take with you, but consider the ideas of those who do not attend the arrangement meeting. Include children in the arrangement decisions - they are grieving too. Let the funeral home know your wishes regarding the presence of the media.

7. **Many times in a traumatic death, law enforcement is involved.** Try to be as cooperative as possible with them. You may be assigned a victim's advocate to work with you and guide you through the court process. Select someone close to you to be with you as you work with the authorities.

8. **During the first few weeks and months, there will be many practical matters to attend to.** Sit down with a friend or family member and make a list of all the things you feel you need to do. Having someone else do this with you helps ensure some things are not forgotten. Go through each item and decide whether it need immediate attention or is something that can wait Making a list is a good way of clarifying the "must do" from the "ought to do".

9. **Experiencing the traumatic death of a loved one often leaves close family and friends also in a state of trauma.** Trauma is different than grief and must be dealt with before dealing with grief. The signs of trauma and grief sometimes intermingle. It is helpful to talk to someone who has experienced a traumatic death or read something about *it*.

10. **When the numbness and shock begin to fade, emotions begin to surface.** It may be weeks or even months after the death. While this is a time when you may need more support it may be less as family and friends take less notice and move on with their lives.

Adapted from: *What to do When the Police Leave: A Guide to the First Days of Traumatic Loss*, Bill Jenkins, 1999, WBJ Press, Richmond, VA

Common Reactions Experienced After A Traumatic Event or Loss

Please note that following a traumatic event, people commonly experience a number of reactions that may seem negative and not feel normal. The following lists reflect normal reactions to these traumatic experiences.

Physical Effects
- Fatigue, exhaustion
- Increased physical pain
- Sleep disturbances
- Cardiovascular strain
- Reduced immune response
- Decreased appetite
- Decreased libido
- Hyperarousal
- Nausea
- Dizziness
- Headaches
- Gastrointestinal problems
- Increased startle response
- Muscle tremors
- Profuse sweating
- Digestive problems
- Somatic complaints
- Ritualistic behavior
- More accident prone

Emotional Effects
- Shock
- Fear/terror
- Irritability
- Anger
- Grief or sadness
- Depression
- Despair
- Loss of pleasure from familiar activities
- Nervousness
- Blame
- Guilt
- Emotional Numbing
- Helplessness
- Identification with the victim
- Difficulty feeling happy

Interpersonal Effects
- Increased relational conflict
- Reduced relational intimacy
- Impaired work performance
- Impaired school performance
- Feeling abandoned/rejected
- Social withdrawal
- Alienation
- Decreased satisfaction
- Distrust
- Externalization of blame
- Externalization of vulnerability
- Over protectiveness

Cognitive Effects
- Impaired concentration
- Impaired decision-making ability
- Memory impairment
- Disbelief
- Confusion
- Distortion
- Self-blame
- Decreased self-esteem
- Decreased self-efficacy
- Worry
- Dissociation (e.g., tunnel vision, dreamlike or "spacey" feeling

Spiritual Effects
- Spiritual disconnection with God
- Questioning God and theological beliefs
- Anger at God
- Spiritual emptiness
- Withdrawal from the faith community
- Increased awareness of morality
- Guilt for feelings, i.e. anger, desire for vengeance
